Cambridge **Discovery Education**™

▶ **INTERACTIVE READERS**

Series editor: Bob Hastings

CATCH A WAVE

THE STORY OF SURFING

A1

Genevieve Kocienda

CAMBRIDGE
UNIVERSITY PRESS

Discovery
EDUCATION™

CAMBRIDGE UNIVERSITY PRESS
Cambridge, New York, Melbourne, Madrid, Cape Town,
Singapore, São Paulo, Delhi, Mexico City

Cambridge University Press
32 Avenue of the Americas, New York, NY 10013-2473, USA

www.cambridge.org
Information on this title: www.cambridge.org/9781107651913

© Cambridge University Press 2014

First published 2014

Printed in Hong Kong, China, by Golden Cup Printing Company Limited

A catalog record for this publication is available from the British Library.

Library of Congress Cataloging-in-Publication Data

Kocienda, G.
  Catch a wave : the story of surfing : level A1 / Genevieve Kocienda.
     pages cm. -- (Cambridge discovery interactive readers)
  ISBN 978-1-107-65191-3 (pbk. : alk. paper)
  1. Surfing--Juvenile literature. I. Title.

GV839.55.K63 2014
797.3'2--dc23

                              2013025117

ISBN 978-1-107-65191-3

Additional resources for this publication at www.cambridge.org

Layout services, art direction, book design, and photo research: Q2ABillSMITH GROUP
Editorial services: Hyphen S.A.
Audio production: CityVox, New York
Video production: Q2ABillSMITH GROUP

Contents

Before You Read:
Get Ready!

Many people like to sit on the beach and watch the water. But some people want to do something more exciting!

Look at the pictures. Then complete the sentences below with the correct words.

fall

sand

surf

surfboard

waves

wetsuit

1 Children like to play in the _____ at the beach.

2 On some beaches, the _____ are very big.

3 A good _____ is long and can be very expensive.

4 It's not easy to learn to _____ but it's fun.

5 A _____ helps you stay warm in cold water.

6 When people surf, they often _____ into the water.

Read the paragraph. Then complete the sentences below with the correct highlighted words.

I like to swim in the ocean in the summer. I live near the coast, so it is very easy to go to the beach in my free time. The beach near my house is really beautiful. It's a very popular place to go. Many people like to surf there. I like to watch them. They lie face down on their surfboards and paddle with their arms out into the water. They float on the water and wait for a good wave. They stand up and try to keep their balance. And then they surf.

1. It's hard to _____ a boat with your arms.
2. Some people find it hard to keep their _____ when they ride a bike.
3. Surfing is very _____ in Australia and Hawaii.
4. There are some beautiful beaches on the _____ of California.
5. Between the United States and Japan is the Pacific _____ .
6. Surfboards _____ on the water.

Comparatives

Use the words in the box to complete the paragraph.

good	better	best

Sara is a **1** _____ swimmer, but Selena swims **2** _____ than Sara. William is the **3** _____ swimmer of all.

CHAPTER 1

The Duke

SOME PEOPLE LIKE TO RIDE HORSES OR DRIVE FAST CARS. AND OTHER PEOPLE LIKE TO RIDE WAVES.

People started surfing a long time ago. In the 1400s, people in the group of islands we now call Hawaii surfed as a sport. But one person made surfing famous. His name was Duke Kahanamoku.

Duke was born in Honolulu, Hawaii, in 1890. When he was a boy, he loved swimming and surfing. He also liked sleeping. In 1912, at the Olympics in Stockholm, Sweden, he fell asleep[1] before his **race**! Everyone had to wait while he put on his **swimsuit**. He swam very fast. He **broke the world record**. At the 1920 Olympics in Belgium, he broke the world record again.

[1]**fell asleep:** went to sleep

Duke was the most famous Hawaiian in the world.

At that time, surfing was not popular outside of Hawaii. But Duke showed many people how to surf. In Australia, he made a **surfboard** out of a tree. Then he took a woman, Isabel Latham, on the surfboard with him. She was the first Australian surfer.

Duke showed many people in the United States how to surf, too. People were more and more interested in this fun sport.

Duke had an interesting life and was very popular. He won many swimming races. He was in movies in Hollywood. He started the first surf club[2] in Oahu, Hawaii. And for more than 25 years, he was the sheriff of Honolulu. Today, he is called "the Father of Surfing."

[2]**club:** a group of people who do the same thing together

Duke was the sheriff, or head policeman, of Honolulu.

? **ANALYZE**
Why do you think surfing is popular today?

CHAPTER 2

Hanging Ten

SURFING IS FUN, BUT DIFFICULT. WHAT DO YOU NEED TO KNOW ABOUT SURFING?

Very good surfers can "hang ten." That is, they can surf with both their feet – all ten toes – at the front of the surfboard. This is not easy. Before you hang ten, you have to learn a lot.

First, a new surfer has to choose the right surfboard. It should be long and **thick** because a long, thick surfboard floats very well. It helps you **keep your balance** on the **waves**.

Next, you have to choose the right place. A good place for a new surfer is a flat,[3] sandy beach. It's good if it isn't busy. You don't want to hit other surfers with your surfboard. And, you don't want their surfboards to hit you!

[3] **flat:** no hills or high places

Video Quest

Wetsuits

Watch this video to learn about why surfers need wetsuits. How does a wetsuit keep you warm?

What do you wear when you surf? You can wear a swimsuit, but in cold water, a wetsuit is best. A wetsuit keeps your body warm so you can be in the water for a long time.

The first thing you must practice before you begin to surf is "popping up." You put your surfboard down on the sand. Next, you **lie** on it with your face down. Then you get up onto your feet very fast, or "pop up." You must practice this many times before you take your surfboard into the **ocean**.

First, lie on your surfboard.

1. Wax your surfboard. 2. Put the leash on your leg.

You are almost ready to go into the ocean and ride those waves. OK, only very small ones! But there are two more things to do.

First, you must wax the top of your surfboard. This is so your feet don't slip.[4] Then, you must put the leash from your surfboard on your leg. You are going to fall, and you don't want to lose your surfboard.

Now you can "get wet" – this is surfer language for getting in the water with your surfboard. You paddle out into the water, behind where the waves break. When you see a wave come, paddle until the wave is under the surfboard, and then pop up. Ride the wave straight to the beach. You surfed!

[4]**slip:** When your foot slips on something, you fall.

3. Find where the waves break.

4. If you're good, surf a tube!

Good surfers want a long ride. They don't surf straight to the beach. That is a short ride. They surf across the water from one side to the other and ride the "face" of the wave. If the surfers are very good, and practice for many years, they can ride inside the "tube" of a big wave.

How do you know if there are good waves for you to surf? Go on your computer! Many popular surf beaches have surfcams. These are video cameras that show how high and how fast the waves are.

Now get wet, practice a lot, and maybe you can hang ten!

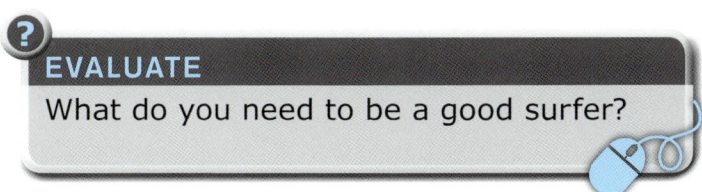

EVALUATE
What do you need to be a good surfer?

CHAPTER 3

Surfer's Paradise

YOU CAN SURF ON BEAUTIFUL BEACHES
ALL AROUND THE WORLD.

Many surfers want to surf the waves at Pipeline in Oahu, Hawaii. There, the waves are more than six meters high. Oahu is the most famous surfing place in the world, but it's very dangerous. Sometimes the best surfers get hurt or die here.

Another dangerous place is Mavericks in California, USA. Only the best surfers try to surf here. You can't paddle out because the waves are too high and too strong. Someone has to take you out to the waves with a jet ski. Then, you wait for one of the 25-meter waves and try not to fall. A very good surfer, Mark Foo, died here in 1994.

For a very long ride, surfers go to Jeffreys Bay, South Africa. The waves there are called Supertubes. Very good surfers can ride these waves for 300 meters.

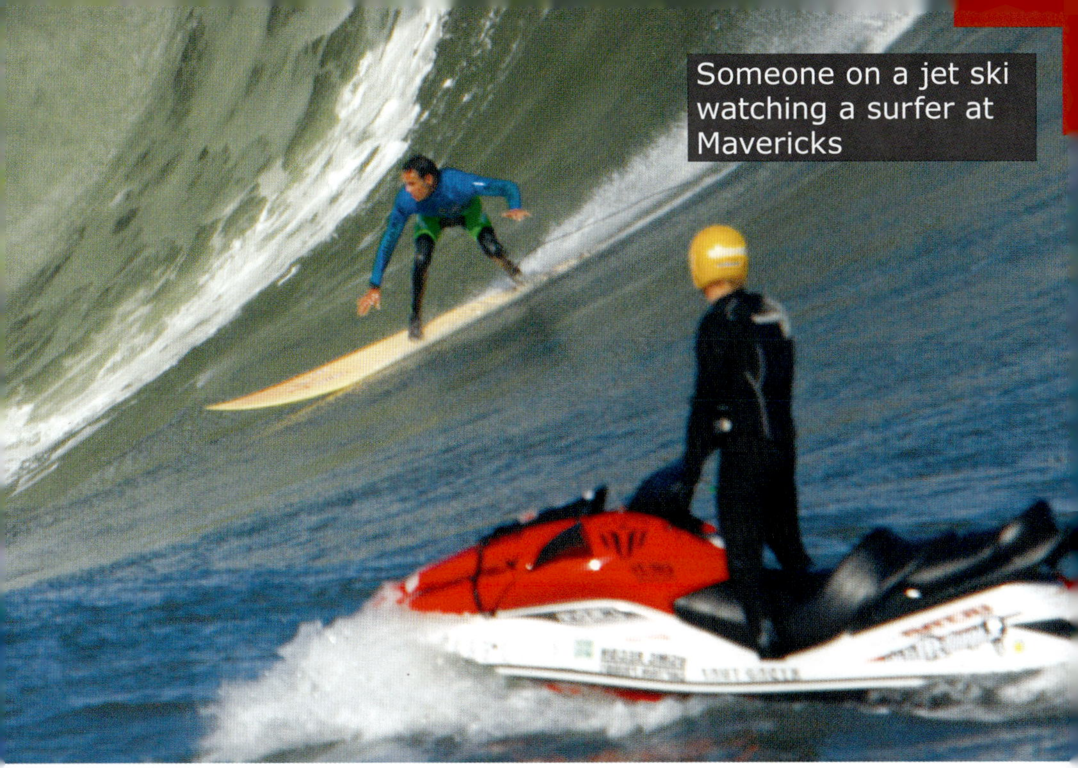

Someone on a jet ski watching a surfer at Mavericks

In Europe, the best place to surf is Hossegor, near Biarritz, France. Many popular surf beaches are near small, sleepy towns, but not Hossegor. In 1854, Napoleon III and his wife, Empress Eugénie, had a very large house there. Today, the rich[5] and famous live there, too.

You can surf in the morning and look for movie stars on the beach in the afternoon. Then in the evening, eat fantastic French food and go to sleep in Napoleon's house – today, it's a hotel!

Hossegor, France

[5]**rich:** having a lot of money

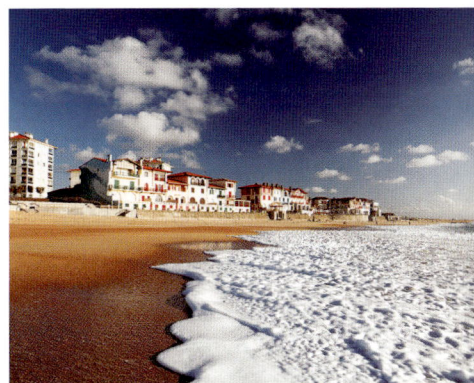

Garrett McNamara
surfing in Portugal

Portugal is a good place to watch surfing. The waves are much too high for most surfers. In January 2013, Hawaiian surfer Garrett McNamara surfed a 30-meter wave off the coast of Nazaré. That may be the world record for the highest wave surfed!

Did you know you can see the Statue of Liberty and go surfing on the same day? There's a good surf beach in Montauk, only three hours from New York City by train.

Or how about riding a camel to the beach? The coast of Morocco is next to the hot, dry Sahara Desert. There are not a lot of surf towns or hotels along the coast. Some people bring their own food and water and everything they need. But the waves are some of the best in the world.

How about surfing near a jungle? On Tamarindo Beach in Costa Rica, you can hear monkeys and toucans as you wait for the next wave. And the water is warm, so you won't need a wetsuit.

A toucan

Gold Coast, Australia

The Gold Coast of Australia is one of the best places in the world to surf, for good surfers and for new ones, too. Maybe it's the place for you!

Video Quest

Lifeguard Competition

Watch this video to learn about a special competition in Australia. What do the lifeguards do at the competition?

COLUMBIA PICTURES presents

The Endless Summer

CHAPTER 4

TECHNICOLOR

Surf Culture

SUN, SWIMSUITS, AND SURFING!

Most people can't surf on a surfboard made from a tree like Duke Kahanamoku did. So, in the 1920s, some people made new, bigger surfboards. These boards floated well and were easier for surfers to use.

And, more people had cars. It was easier to take a surfboard from beach to beach in California and look for good waves. So, more people started surfing.

Two Hollywood movies showed this new surfer culture[6] to the world.

[6] **culture:** the music, clothes, language, etc., of a group of people

In 1959, *Gidget* showed beautiful young men and women having fun, falling in love, going to the beach, and surfing. Many young people in the USA wanted that kind of life. They bought surfboards and swimsuits. The beaches in California and Hawaii were packed![7]

Then, in 1964, *The Endless Summer* came out. This movie was very different from *Gidget*. It shows two men from California looking for the "perfect[8] wave." The men travel to beautiful places all over the world. People wanted to see those places, too.

Today, there are popular surfing movies, too. The 2012 movie *Chasing Mavericks* is about Jay Moriarty. At age 16, he was the youngest person to surf the dangerous Mavericks waves.

[7]**packed:** having many, many people in one place
[8]**perfect:** the best; without anything bad

In the 1960s, surfing music **became** popular. The Beach Boys sang about the California surfing lifestyle with songs like "Surfin' USA" and "Surfer Girl." It was happy, sunny music. The songs were about having fun with friends at the beach, surfing together, and beautiful women in bikinis.[9]

Elvis Presley visited Hawaii a lot, and in 1961, he was a singing surfer in the movie *Blue Hawaii*. Elvis wore colorful Hawaiian-style shirts with big flowers, and soon those shirts became popular outside Hawaii.

[9]**bikini:** a two-piece swimsuit for women

But Hawaiian shirts are just one part of surfer fashion.[10] Surfers wear board shorts, T-shirts with surfing pictures or colorful Hawaiian flowers, and flip flops.

In the late 1950s, surfing culture moved to the streets. Many surfers started surfing the sidewalks[11] on skateboards. They found it had the same feel as riding a wave. Today, there are many different kinds of skateboards. Some of them can help you learn to surf.

Over time, skateboarding culture changed. Today, many skateboarders don't go surfing. But skateboarders and surfers can buy their boards and clothes at the same stores. And both sports use some of the same words. Yes, you can "hang ten" skateboarding, too!

....
[10] **fashion:** a kind of clothing
[11] **sidewalk:** where people walk next to a street

Board shorts ⟶

?
EVALUATE
Why do you think surfing culture is popular with people who don't surf?

Flip flops ⟶

A bodyboarder with fins

CHAPTER 5

What Do You Think?

THERE IS MORE THAN ONE WAY TO SURF.

Bodyboarding

In bodyboarding, or boogie boarding, you lie down on a short board and ride the waves. You don't stand up. Bodyboarders wear fins on their feet. The fins help them swim fast to catch a wave.

Bodysurfing

Your body is the surfboard. Like surfing, you swim out and wait for a wave. The wave comes and you swim very fast. When the wave is under you, put your arms out in front of you and ride. It's easy! But be careful. If a big wave hits you, it is easy to "eat sand"!

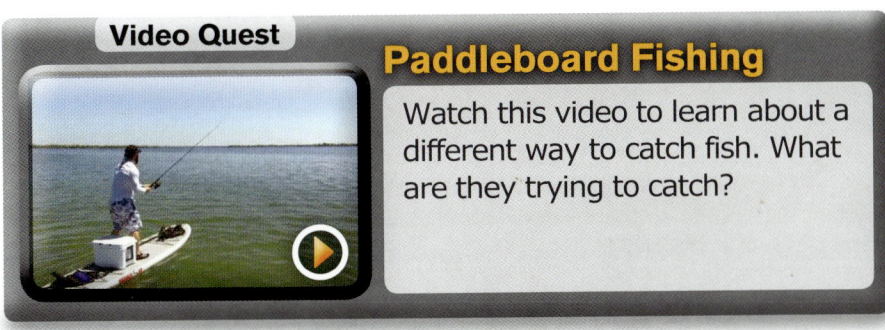

Video Quest

Paddleboard Fishing

Watch this video to learn about a different way to catch fish. What are they trying to catch?

Stand up paddleboard surfing, or SUP

You stand on a paddleboard and paddle with an oar. You don't need waves or the ocean: You can paddleboard in a river. You can go fast or slow, and look at things around you. Paddleboarding is good exercise and easy to do. Many skiers like to paddleboard in the summer when there is no snow.

Windsurfing

The surfboard has a sail on it. You stand on the board and hold the sail with your hands. When it's windy, you can go very fast. The fastest windsurfers can go about 80 kilometers per hour!

What do you think? Surfing, SUP, bodyboarding, windsurfing, or bodysurfing. Did you try any of them? Which one do you want to try?

A windsurfer has a sail.

After You Read

Read the sentences and choose Ⓐ True or Ⓑ False.

1 Duke Kahanamoku was a very fast runner.
   Ⓐ True
   Ⓑ False

2 To "hang ten" means to surf with your feet at the back of the surfboard.
   Ⓐ True
   Ⓑ False

3 A new surfer should use a short surfboard.
   Ⓐ True
   Ⓑ False

4 In cold water, you should wear a wetsuit.
   Ⓐ True
   Ⓑ False

5 Mavericks is the name of a beach with very dangerous waves in California.
   Ⓐ True
   Ⓑ False

6 Supertubes are waves in South Africa.
   Ⓐ True
   Ⓑ False

7 Bodyboarding and boogie boarding are very different sports.
   Ⓐ True
   Ⓑ False

8 A windsurfer uses a sail.
   Ⓐ True
   Ⓑ False

Who's Who?

Match the people with the correct information about them.

1 _____ is called "the Father of Surfing."

2 _____ died at Mavericks.

3 _____ sang about surfing.

4 _____ was in a surfing movie.

5 _____ surfed a 30-meter wave.

a. Garrett McNamara

b. The Beach Boys

c. Mark Foo

d. Duke Kahanamoku

e. Jay Moriarty

Do or See?

Write the words in the box in the correct place in the chart.

| coast | fall | float | ocean | paddle | sand | surf | wave |

Things you can do	Things you can see

Talk About It

A friend wants to go surfing with you. Think about the different surfing places in this book. Which place do you want to go to? Why?

Answer Key

Words to Know, page 4
1 sand **2** waves **3** surfboard **4** surf **5** wetsuit **6** fall

Words to Know, page 5
1 paddle **2** balance **3** popular **4** coast **5** Ocean
6 float

Comparatives, page 5
1 good **2** better **3** best

Analyze, page 7 *Answers will vary.*

Video Quest, page 9
The wetsuit keeps the surfer warm by letting just a little bit of water inside. The water can't get out, so it gets hotter and keeps the body warm.

Evaluate, page 11 *Answers will vary.*

Video Quest, page 15
The lifeguards have surfing races.

Evaluate, page 19 *Answers will vary.*

Video Quest, page 21
A shark

True or False?, page 22
1 B **2** B **3** B **4** A **5** A **6** A **7** B **8** A

Who's Who?, page 23
1 d **2** c **3** b **4** e **5** a

Do or See?, page 23
Do: fall, float, paddle, surf; See: coast, ocean, sand, wave

Talk About It, page 23 *Answers will vary.*